Like a Flash Eclipse

Also by Elizabeth Goodsir
Wind Rippling Water
Blue Pollen Beautiful
It Can Take Till Now

Elizabeth Goodsir
Like a Flash Eclipse

To Janet Grecian and Chris Pearce
holders of words and readers and writers
with love and gratitude
for such long-time generosity and support

To Stephen and Brenda
Thank you for your open-hearted gifts of support
and professionalism.
And congratulations Stephen on being awarded the Medal of
the Order of Australia, 2021, for your twenty-five-year
service to publishing. Hear us all clapping and cheering with
pride and gratitude at the wonder of Ginninderra Press.

Like a Flash Eclipse
ISBN 978 1 76109 137 7
Copyright © Elizabeth Goodsir 2021

First published 2021 by
Ginninderra Press
PO Box 3461 Port Adelaide 5015
www.ginninderrapress.com.au

Contents

Biding	9
January	10
Darkness	11
Exchanging	12
Grandfather	13
He ceased	14
Daybreak	15
Horizons	16
In resonance	17
Stripping	18
A better guise	19
Perhaps in parting	20
Losing	21
Dusk at last	22
Ocean	23
Easing	24
I watched her	25
Heartbreak	27
Peep of day	28
The river	29
The heart	30
Beseech	31
This morning	32
Alone	33
Even though	34
From Knocklofty's Peak	35
At Uluru	36
All day long	38
Moonlight came	39
Unheeding of damp skies	40

I see time	41
Morning grain	42
An Affair	43
As we sat	44
After the playground	45
Like a hawk	46
And I say to my son	47
Sirens wind	48
Flirt and flicker	49
Hour by hour you leave	50
Wind chimes	51
Hardly here	52
Camouflage	53
Flee	54
It's all right	55
Light rained	56
The green scalloped plate	57
We try	58
Australia burns, 2020	59
How big must it get, this bag of memory	60
It's kind this fraying porous me	61
Post-burn	62
Postscript	64

When the moon is full
it begins to wane

The year of

wildfire
family change and challenge
last days
and the magic friendship of birds

Loss of self
loss of other
like fire
reduces
rekindles

Biding

a summer of challenge   reconcile
of space and trust

a whirl wind of question and fire
newness and chance

till the days shorten
and darkness thickens

autumn stillness
settles and softens

soon winter will
bury and redeem

January

like raging   hot-poker anger
the fire crackled and snapped
moved across the earth's body
red and new
ready to kill

towering flames of leaping orange
roared up timber
jumped the chasms
filled the canyons with trapped smoke
squeezing air from homes and lungs

Darkness

lies upon your face
diagnosis drifts away
as you nudge the crowding future
with resolve

your deep quiet
not the silence of grief
more like music
resting

Exchanging

glances
feeling the pain
the sun strips
each word
from the room
burning silent white
into every corner

Grandfather

pine trees cast shadow
on burning wishes
deafening sparrows
joined the frenzy

words flew like shuttlecocks
wreaking havoc in the heart
if only I could clip their wings

from your silent chair
you made stillness
deadening the heart screech
hushing chafed throats

a pigeon balloons its throat
I'm filed with new breath

although tired to the bone
pure sun infects

every cell with dance
even dragging feet skip a step

He ceased

to exist when
he hit the shore

all that swelling and tumbling
and crashing and arriving

to nothing
invisible

short-lived
like a wave

yet still
entangled

consumed by
the receding tide

he re-forms in
the endless turmoil

intimate   unflinching
immortal

Daybreak

morning of pale blue
we lean into its firm bite

to the habit of predicting
imagining

two morning birds listening
not speaking to each other

taking it in turns to hear
the other's song

precious morning
lesson

Horizons

in silence and tears
in needing to chill the heart
and cool the kiss

our heart begins its tearing
fractures the shared mountain climbs
the side-by-side waiting

to sit in unknown waters
freedom too big to fathom
endless raw material

slowly bending to notice
new beauty
a different path winding gladly

In resonance

the breeze at sunrise
murmured new day promises

tugged at old sadness
like pulling weeks

it rippled the garden
of inner glory

releasing the heart to blow
in the spreading dawn

Stripping

reckless greed
slurps and spews
hurls weapon after weapon

victim and victor

lives splintered
rubbed   rocked
torn and looted

roaring terror

stones flame and crack
tongues lick and fling and suck
inside out

on and on

where is mercy

A better guise

he dreamed of going back
where they could talk and see
each other in the right manner

a moment when his lived life
passed away and he was
given another fate

where pain and nonsense
turned into gleanings
to harvest and winnow

leftovers that he could bake
into a new loaf
solid and hearty and risen

he dreamed they lived simply
on this earth   a blessed acre
of love and honour

photos children and
their children took pride in
things he made – used and worn

no longer an approximation
truly unfeigned   faithful
heartfelt

Perhaps in parting

we have merely
slipped into the next room

whatever we were to each
other we still are

in more space we
allow the fullness

take back the
shadow we cast

are grateful for
other dreams

for the loneliness that
cherishes companionship

and frees the secret
undiscovered self

Losing

is not hard to master

many things seem
intent on being lost

or is that we stop
insisting they be found

Dusk at last

the day faded
colourless
so easy to miss
if only we had

the evening long and hard
until sleepy voices
call for one more story
one more kiss

and it's easy to promise
tomorrow's new day

Easing

at the dinner table
drop by drop
water glasses
fill with laughter

I watched her

brave   constant   smiling
doing what was agreed

timetables   pick-up   handing over
trying not to listen
to the old banter

she had wanted this end
to incessant blame
sticky guilt

too long sickened
with her own
disappointment

but the heartbreak was helpless
came and went
of its own accord

invaded time
promised rest could not be
walked around   ignored   refused

other pieces of life took up
their new shape
but not heartbreak

it stamped all over
bargains
wanting consolations

insisted the losses hurt
unpreventable
consuming

despite giving it time
it wanted more time
not time to reach the end

rather the allowing for
deep caring
to lose control

to be broken open to
the inevitable   the inescapable
letting be

Ocean

tosses itself on the beach
lies on the sand
rocks   idles

windswept
it sprays and flings
chases

grabbed by the moon
silvered and struck
grain by grain it slips silently

Heartbreak

is the beautifully helpless
side of love that takes
time to let go

Peep of day

moon lays shadows beneath the walnut tree
bursts open the heavy scent of fig
leaves whisper like straying angels
and tenderness of long ago days

birds laugh in rhymes and frenzied delight
singe their wings on the crack of dawn
fall out of time like berries dripping juice
fill my cup with today's donations

The river

spread like glass
evening clouds sleep on still water
and across our windless faces

The heart

is reckless and heedless
in its desire to love
mindlessly   deeply
it craves to grow

erratic   hot   fast
it fans and flares
till the fire has run its course
no tingle in the pain   no thirst in the burn

in the blackened aftermath
it breaks apart to breathe
and allow light for new shoots
to wander in the ruins

Beseech

dear home engulfed by sea
what have we done
to let your mountains
and grasses   gullies
and forests burn so
unrelentlessly

dare we pray for
drops from
tender clouds

This morning

you stand still
hold your breath
arriving
arriving after such a long flight
into your new story

Alone

is always there
it doesn't come
with sleepless night
failure
threat

it's when we feel
that we can't
fulfil
the needs of
the human heart

yet it is what
takes us to the
heart of our humanity
to our seeking
our home within

Even though

shaken like a mouse
in a lion's mouth
belief never left him
he sang to the children of rapture

From Knocklofty's Peak

under a wide morning sky
to where the gums arch and meet

and the sun is patterned and weak
throwing silhouettes and shadows

the river spreads smooth
blue green then golden brown

straying clouds catch a current
the sun all-consuming again

this perfect day without
before or after

made for me

not another soul
knows this moment

so much more than
autumn skies   dawn-still waters

At Uluru

as the sun played
on the rock's smooth face
the beauty of evening climbed
melting its face
in deep violet darkness
day had fallen   birds were hushed

and I thought of our children
like the sun scaling to its
greatest height
steady and bright
discovering
its significance

they too
rise   fill   expand
to their greatest goals
then like the sun
on the stroke of noon
begin their conversion

reversing values and ideals
cherished in the morning
to questions   confusion
afternoon challenges

one by one they choose
to name themselves
free fall like wayward stars
trusting their own destiny
will call them to who they really are

from my Nightfall
I watch them unfold into
their deep truth
their holy courage
and wonder at the
beauty of the afternoon

All day long

the lace-edged sea goes

in and out
in and out

marking time
marking time

I breathe the
ceaseless change

Moonlight came

and emptied me of self
every vein and every pore

made me into a container
to be filled by love

all there is
is to stay that way

no questions
no answers

Unheeding of damp skies

flaring and trembling
might ignites
combusts   explodes
hunts down
till there is no more

like a flash eclipse
unreasonably   morbidly
black ash smoulders
sleeping and cool
death stillness

I see time

slowly heal heart wounds
and in their place fine lines of hope and light

deep courage in labored steps
new naming   no knowns

such credence in
another way

Morning grain

they watch as I corner the stairs
to the kitchen

open doors onto dewy grass
take down the jar of grain

sliding along the wall
chatting their new-day greeting

shuffling and bickering
if I take too long

they drop at last to the scattered meal
each of us grateful to be doing it one more time

An affair

all day long I strive to do unmeasurable things
love the unknown   the world   God

say yes to everything I don't understand
ask questions not needing answers

plant seeds I will not harvest
notice endings and smile

make tracks in the wrong
direction

trust my joy will not
disturb other's sleep

entangle until
I am one

As we sat

in the rawness
of wondering
their summer bodies
slipped into the sea
wrapping us in salty laughter

After the playground

they worried which house

does it matter
there are cradles
of eider down and
warm honey milk
in both

Like a hawk

I watch their metamorphosis
wondering what's taking

place within the chrysalis
what has to unthicken
lengthen   disintegrate

how long in the dark
the cool   self-spun web
of hope and trust

how long to be born
to new possibilities
and powers

is birthing ever over
I remind myself
to wonder

And I say to my son

we have to lose all we hold
and count and save

and know desolate
sorrow-filled landscapes

to feel the delicate threads
of care and attention

both deep inside
and waving from the crowd

and he answers

I'm grateful to be
meeting all of myself

Sirens wind

the hours
into one
heart-aching
prayer

If only the sea spray
circling the entire island
could dissolve this
coast to coast flame

perhaps darkness
will wipe away
such sadness
like a mother's
knowing apron

Flirt and flicker

dipping and dancing
insisting on priority and place
full and flight-ready

after bath-splash and splatter
fluffing and brushing
balancing

a call from
their deep black
throats

wings them
clean to the
setting sun

Hour by hour you leave

when noon is nestling in the summer leaves
I see your shadow dappled and dancing

by afternoon clouds heave and roll
and tumble you like an umbrella in ocean wind

moonlight renders you so weightless and ageless
there is nothing left to take away

Wind chimes

to see the shattered
plate glass life
broken a million times
now making
music from a
leafy bough

Hardly here

behind closed eyes
I feel you

scouting between now and there
leaving your bed to check the other place

I sense you smiling
at the truth of it all

perhaps more there
than here now

are you laughing at the dream
we live here on earth

is the wonder of such wakefulness
so stunning that you wish

you could startle us
all into knowing there

Camouflage

From our night window
the cry of a tawny frogmouth

this morning I passed it widely
honouring its mimicry

head pointed upwards
silver grey plumage patterned

into the form of a broken
tree branch

whispering to its chick
to stay day-silent

Flee

paws   claws
run   leap   hop
not fast enough for
the melting earth

such hurt black faces
tired   alive
hand   heart
outreaching

broken whispers
of disbelief
still believing

It's all right

that my former lives are departing
loss of hearing helps them leave
like flocks of birds

left is space and
silence and time
to describe in the quiet

and still I will only have
used a pinhead
of the gifts I received

Light rained

on golden floorboards
washing them white
if only so much ash
was made of mere light

The green scalloped plate

lost its tea set name

like the last of our
beaten silver wedding spoons

nothing belongs now
nothing matches

everything tells its own tale
and we add ours

how long till we
don't notice

don't know
don't mind

We try

You cannot put a fire out
a thing that can ignite
can go, itself, without a fan
upon the slowest night

Emily Dickinson

But how we try

lives on line to save lives
dodging and darting
death   disaster

self-sacrificing   protecting
four from our shores
three from abroad

how we try
against greed
political cowardice

Australia burns, 2020

Climate change?

33 human lives lost
1 billion animals killed
Fifteen and three-quarter million acres torched
Over one and a half thousand homes destroyed

We'll discuss it when it's over

How big must it get, this bag of memory

how big before it splits or leaks

how much more can it grow me
remember me from held baby

ink-stained schoolgirl
lover   spouse   mother

perhaps like a supermarket bag
it carries and empties

lies in wait
until recycled

It's kind   this fraying   porous me

comfy in the thin wornness

the edges ebb and flow
spill and overflow

no need to stand erect on
some belief

firm to a path
a promise

my melting shadow
returning the gift

a crescent moon
free to disappear

Post-burn

hot on heels of nature
I fall in love
with its blackened self

bone-dry skeletons
lace and shell
and seeds

still knowing
to give
once more

Heart pierced as clean
as a carpenter's nail

with that shout of pain
pang of newness

Postscript

These poems were sent for publication at the beginning of the year 2020, and at a time of personal turning, transitioning, transforming.

They speak of loss and change and tragedy, of shame and grief and selfish greed, of courage and deep belief.

But more was to come. Towards the middle of the year, people across the world took a stand against police violence and racism, joined a united struggle for truth, humanity and justice.

In the same months, Covid-19 struck every corner of our planet. Catastrophic numbers of lives were lost; there were long-term illness and disability, unmeasurable economic consequences for individuals, communities, places of work, worlwide uncertainty and trepidation.

Again and again, the weeks exposed inequality, injustice, oppression. Blessedly, many have seen this as the final call for a new understanding, a loud and insistent invitation to each one of us to take action, to challenge, unite and inspire change, to stand with those calling for a fairer future and give a voice to the oppressed and neglected, to use this global crisis to remember what it is to be human.

I had a dream that we realised we had joined a great, new, invisible community encompassing all cultures, enriched by the belonging to all times, all nations, all languages.

All day long.

www.ingramcontent.com/pod-product-compliance
Lightning Source LLC
Chambersburg PA
CBHW062200100526
44589CB00014B/1884